Martin Luther

95 Theses

Disputation of Doctor Martin Luther on the
Power and Efficacy of Indulgences (1517)

with an introduction by
DR. KEN R. SCHURB

CONCORDIA PUBLISHING HOUSE · SAINT LOUIS

This revised edition © 2016 Concordia Publishing House
3558 S. Jefferson Ave., St. Louis, MO 63118-3968
1-800-325-3040 • www.cph.org

English translation from the 1983 edition of Luther's Ninety-Five Theses
Edited by Scot A. Kinnaman

Manufactured in the United States of America

INTRODUCTION

On January 15, 2009, a passenger jet left New York's LaGuardia Airport. Shortly after takeoff, it hit a flock of birds, disabling both of its engines. Despite the lack of thrust, the airliner's captain successfully guided his craft to a safe landing in the Hudson River. Few people had heard of that pilot, Captain Chesley "Sully" Sullenberger, before, but he became an overnight sensation.

Five centuries ago, something similar happened to a little-known Augustinian friar, Martin Luther. It occurred when he nailed his Ninety-Five Theses, composed in Latin, to the door of the Castle Church in Wittenberg.

Quite a Sensation

Of course, electronic media did not exist during Luther's time. Yet through the cutting-edge communication technology of the day, printing via Gutenberg's movable type, Luther became well-known very quickly. Within a month or so, his Theses had been copied and translated into the language of the common people and were being discussed in other German cities. Luther, a thirty-four-year-old priest and professor of theology at the relatively new University of Wittenberg, was turning into quite a sensation.

Unlike Captain Sullenberger's nifty flying, Luther's posting of the Theses had not, in itself, been particularly heroic. The church door served as a sort of public bulletin board, especially for the university. Luther's Theses were propositions for academic discussion, the kind of thing that makes a lot of people yawn.

Luther never got the discussion he wanted. What followed was the Reformation. In fact, the Reformation is usually marked as beginning when Luther posted his Theses on October 31, 1517.

Indulgences

During the previous month, Wittenberg had seen a "Disputation against Scholastic Theology," based on another set of theses by Luther. Many might indeed have yawned at this intellectual exercise. But people took notice when Luther turned to the very practical matter of indulgences.

Indulgences formed part of the penitential system. The church had defined the "sacrament of penance" as consisting of three elements:

1. Confession (resulting from contrition, sorrow over sin)

2. Absolution

3. Satisfaction through self-sacrificing deeds

Penitents needed to be freed not only from the guilt of their sin but also from temporal penalties incurred by their sin, and the church said these penalties would still have to be endured as satisfactions both in this world and beyond in purgatory. Purgatory was not hell, but a horrible, painful place of "purging," where Christian souls were thought to remain for a time after death instead of immediately being with Christ in heaven (Luke 23:43). None knew just how long their own time of purgation was supposed to last.

Via indulgences, one could render satisfaction in a different way. Years before Luther, it became possible to buy indulgences as the third step in penance. The church had come to count on these payments of money as revenue sources, which struck disgruntled folk in German lands and elsewhere as no secret. They were getting tired of their money flowing to Rome.

The most sought after of all indulgences was the "plenary" (full) indulgence, which was claimed to remit all temporal punishments, even for Christians who had died and were putatively in purgatory. The idea had developed that the good works of Christ and the saints numbered more than they needed and formed a "treasury of merits," and indulgence payments could transfer their surplus merits to people in purgatory. Purchase of a plenary indulgence for such a loved one was thought to spring that soul into heaven immediately.[1] Whether buying an indulgence for someone else or oneself, it became easy, Luther later recalled, to imagine that "the grace from indulgences was the same grace as that by which a man is reconciled to God."[2]

---

[1]   See Thesis 27.
[2]   LW 41:232

These precise assertions were made by Johann Tetzel, a Dominican monk who was selling plenary indulgences not far from Wittenberg in the fall of 1517. Some proceeds of his sales went to building St. Peter's Basilica in Rome. The sale had full approval from the pope and from Luther's more immediate ecclesiastical superior, Archbishop Albert of Mainz, who also benefited from the proceeds.

Luther's Ninety-Five Theses

Luther was convinced that the pope could never have authorized something like this. People in Wittenberg—his parishioners—were buying Tetzel's indulgences and thinking that they no longer had to be sorry for their sins. Who needed contrition if they had already "paid in advance"?

Something must be done, Luther thought. He wrote the Ninety-Five Theses.

The Theses started with penance: "Our Lord and Master Jesus Christ, when He said 'repent,' intended that the whole life of believers should be one of repentance."[3] From his study of the Greek, Luther understood that repentance was more than participating in the formal sacrament of penance; it meant a life of penitential actions.

This put indulgences into perspective. They were not to take precedence over works of love for one's neighbor, subsequent Theses went on to say, nor were they to eclipse the grace of God. As Luther eventually put it, "The gospel, which is, after all, the only true indulgence, had to keep silence in the churches in deference to the indulgence."[4]

Yet in 1517, Luther still had much to learn about the biblical Gospel. By his own admission, at the time he did not want to take "a syllable from obedience to the pope."[5] Luther was challenging various aspects of indulgences, particularly indulgences for the dead, but he had not yet thoroughly rejected indulgences.[6] Nor did his Theses question purgatory. Some of them actually ran contrary to the Gospel: "True contrition seeks and loves punishment" or "For by a work of charity, charity increases and man becomes better."[7] Even when he included the pointed query, "What does the pope remit or grant to those who by perfect contrition have a right to full

---

3   Thesis 1
4   LW 34:16
5   LW 34:328
6   See Theses 71, 73, and 91.
7   Theses 40, 44

remission and participation?" Luther came to understand that he was granting too much to contrition while overlooking the forgiving Gospel of Christ as received through faith.[8] By 1520, he wished all his booklets on indulgences would be burned.[9] That would include his first writing on the subject, the Ninety-Five Theses.

Enduring Value

Yet these Theses have enduring value. They began with attention to the biblical text, the word *repent*. In the ensuing controversy, Luther grew more and more to depend on God's Word, the Bible (*sola Scriptura!*), against ecclesiastical authorities like popes or councils.

The diligent biblical study that moved Luther to write the Ninety-Five Theses both resulted from and served as fuel for his personal devotion, his professorial work, and his pastoral interest in the care of souls—starting with his own. The Theses reflected his concern for certainty of salvation. As stated in what has been called the noblest of these Theses, "the true treasure of the Church is the most Holy Gospel of the glory and grace of God."[10]

The Ninety-Five Theses formed a beginning. Luther went on to dig even further into his study of the biblical Gospel. Later he mused over how the Lord had been guiding him since the controversy over indulgences.

Luther had aimed to launch a discussion. To the extent that any discussion includes the genuine Gospel of Christ, it contains God's saving power (Romans 1:16), which really cannot be contained. Not even after five hundred years!

---

[8] Thesis 87
[9] LW 36:11–12
[10] Thesis 62

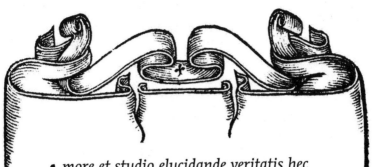

A more et studio elucidande veritatis hec
subscripta disputabuntur Wittenberge,
Presidente R. P. Martino Lutther, Artium
et S. Theologie Magistro eiusdemque ibidem
lectore Ordinario. Quare petit, ut qui non
possunt verbis presentes nobiscum disceptare
agant id literis absentes.

O ut of love for the truth and the desire to bring
it to light, the following propositions will be
debated at Wittenberg, under presidency of the
Reverend Father Martin Luther, Master of Arts and
of Sacred Theology, and the Lecturer on Ordinary
on the same at that place. For that reason, he
requests that those who cannot be present and
debate orally with us may do so by letter.

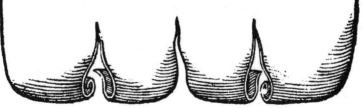

An English Translation of the Ninety-Five Theses

In the name of our Lord Jesus Christ. Amen.

1. Our Lord and Master Jesus Christ, when He said "repent," intended that the whole life of believers should be one of repentance.

2. This word "repent" cannot be understood to mean sacramental penance, that is, of the confession and satisfaction that is administered under the ministry of priests.

3. However, it does not refer solely to inward repentance; no, there is no inward repentance that does not outwardly produce various mortifications of the flesh.

4. The penalty [of sin] continues as long as hatred of self—that is, true inward repentance—continues until our entrance into the kingdom of heaven.

5. The pope has neither the will nor the power to remit any penalties other than those he has imposed either by his own authority or by that of the canons[11].

6. The pope has no power to remit any guilt except by declaring and showing it to have been remitted by God; or, at most, he may grant remission in cases reserved to his judgment, for if his power in such cases were despised, the guilt would certainly remain.

7. God remits guilt to no one whom He does not, at the same time, humble in all things, bringing him into subjection to the authority of His representative, the priest.

8. The penitential canons are imposed only upon the living, and, according to them, no burden should be imposed on the dying.

9. Therefore, the Holy Spirit acting in the pope does well for us, because in his decrees he always makes exception of the article of death and of necessity.

---

[11] Canons: decrees of the church, having the force of law

10. Those priests act wrongly and ignorantly who, in the case of the dying, reserve canonical penances for purgatory.

11. This changing of the canonical penalty into the penalty of purgatory is quite evidently one of the tares[12] that seem to have been sown while the bishops were asleep.

12. Previously, the canonical penalties were imposed not after, but before absolution, as tests of true contrition.

13. The dying are freed by death from all penalties and are already dead to canonical laws and have a right to be released from them.

14. The imperfect health or love of the dying brings with it, of necessity, great fear; and the smaller the love, the greater is the fear.

15. This fear and horror are sufficient by themselves (to say nothing of other things) to constitute the penalty of purgatory, since it is very near to the horror of despair.

16. Hell, purgatory, and heaven seem to differ as do despair, near-despair, and the assurance of safety.

17. For souls in purgatory, it seems necessary that horror should grow less and love increase.

18. It seems unproved, either by any reasoning or by Scripture, that they are outside the state of merit, that is to say, of increasing love.

19. Nor does it appear to be proved that they are certain and confident of their own blessedness, or at least not all of them, though we may be very certain of it.

20. Therefore, when the pope speaks of the "plenary [full] remission of all penalties," he does not actually mean "of all," but only of those imposed by himself.

21. As a result, those indulgence preachers are in error who say that by the pope's indulgences one is free from all punishment and saved.

22. For in fact, he remits to souls in purgatory no penalty that, according to the canons, they would have had to pay in this life.

---

12 Tares: an injurious weed resembling wheat when young (Matthew 13:24–30)

23. If it is at all possible that remission of all penalties whatsoever can be granted to anyone, it is certain that it is granted to none but the most perfect, that is, to very few.

24. For this reason, the greater part of the people are deceived by this indiscriminate and high-sounding promise of release from penalties.

25. The same powers that the pope has over purgatory in general, every bishop has in his own diocese, and in particular, every curate has within his own parish.

26. The pope acts most rightly in granting remission to souls [in purgatory], not by the power of the Keys—which in this case he does not possess—but by way of intercessory prayer.

27. Those who say that as soon as the penny rattles into the money box, the soul flies out [of purgatory], preach only human doctrine.

28. It is certain that when the penny rattles into the money box, gain and avarice can be increased, but the result of the intercession of the Church is in the power of God alone.

29. Who knows whether all the souls in purgatory wish to be redeemed from it in view of what is said of St. Severinus and St. Pascal[13]?

30. No one is sure that his own contrition is sincere; much less that he has attained full remission.

31. One who truly buys indulgences is as rare as a truly penitent man, that is to say, most rare.

32. Those who believe that because they have letters of pardon[14] they are made sure of their own salvation will be condemned eternally along with their teachers.

33. We must be on guard against those who say that the pope's pardons are that inestimable gift of God by which man is reconciled to Him;

34. For the grace conveyed by these pardons concerns only the penalties of sacramental satisfaction, which are of human appointment.

---

[13] This refers to the legend that both Severinus and Pope Paschal I were willing to endure the pains of purgatory in order to benefit the faithful.

[14] Luther uses the terms *pardon* and *indulgences* interchangeably.

35. They preach unchristian doctrine who teach that contrition is not necessary for those who intend to buy souls out of purgatory or to buy confessionalia.[15]

36. Every truly repentant Christian has plenary [full] remission of penalty and guilt, even without letters of pardon.

37. Every true Christian, whether living or dead, has a part in all the benefits of Christ and the Church, given him by God, even without letters of pardon.

38. Nevertheless, the remission and participation granted by the pope is by no means to be despised, since it is, as I have said, the declaration of divine remission.

39. It is most difficult, even for the most learned theologians, to exalt before the people the great riches of indulgences and, at the same time, to commend the necessity of true contrition.

40. True contrition seeks and loves punishment, while liberal pardons only relax penalties and cause them to be hated, or at least gives occasion to do so.

41. Apostolic pardons are to be preached with caution, lest the people falsely suppose that they are to be preferred to other good works of charity.

42. Christians should be taught that the pope does not intend the buying of pardons to be compared in any way to works of mercy.

43. Christians are to be taught that he who gives to the poor or lends to the needy does a better work than buying pardons;

44. For by a work of charity, charity increases and man becomes better; but by indulgences, man does not grow better, only freer from penalties.

45. Christians are to be taught that he who sees anyone in need and passes him by yet gives his money for pardons, is not purchasing the indulgence of the pope, but the indignation of God.

---

[15] Confessionalia: privileges entitling the holder to choose their own confessor and relieving him of certain satisfactions

46. Christians are to be taught that unless they have more than they need, they are bound to keep back what is necessary for their own families, and by no means to squander it on indulgences.

47. Christians are to be taught that buying indulgences is a matter of freedom and not of commandment.

48. Christians should be taught that in granting pardons, the pope needs, and therefore desires, their devout prayer for him more than the money they bring.

49. Christians should be taught that the pope's pardons are useful, if they do not put their trust in them; but altogether harmful, if through them they lose the fear of God.

50. Christians are to be taught that if the pope knew the exactions of the indulgence preachers, he would rather see the Basilica of St. Peter burned to ashes than that it should be built up with the skin, flesh, and bones of his sheep.

51. Christians should be taught that the pope, as is his duty, would rather, if necessary, sell the Basilica of St. Peter and give of his own money to those from whom the indulgence preachers extract money.

52. The hope of salvation by letters of pardon is vain, even though the commissary—no, even the pope himself—were to pledge his own soul for them.

53. They are enemies of Christ and of the pope who bid the Word of God to be altogether silent in some churches in order that pardons may be preached.

54. Injury is done to the Word of God when, in the same sermon, an equal or a longer time is spent on pardons than on this Word.

55. It must be the intention of the pope that if pardons (which is a very small matter) are celebrated with one bell, a single procession, and a single ceremony, then the Gospel (which is the very greatest thing) should be celebrated with a hundred bells, a hundred processions, and a hundred ceremonies.

56. The treasures of the Church, out of which the pope grants indulgences, are not sufficiently named or known among the people of Christ.

57. It is clear that they are not temporal treasures, for many of the vendors do not pour out such treasures so easily, but only accumulate them.

58. Nor are they the merits of Christ and the saints, for even without the pope, these always work grace for the inner man, and the cross, death, and hell for the outward man.

59. St. Lawrence said that the treasures of the Church were the Church's poor, but he spoke according to the usage of the word in his own time.

60. Without rashness we say that the Keys of the Church, given by Christ's merit, are that treasure;

61. For it is clear that for the remission of penalties and of reserved cases, the power of the pope is of itself sufficient.

62. The true treasure of the Church is the most Holy Gospel of the glory and grace of God.

63. But this treasure naturally arouses hatred, for it makes the first to be last.

64. On the other hand, the treasure of indulgences is naturally most acceptable, for it makes the last to be first.

65. Therefore, the treasures of the Gospel are nets with which they were formerly accustomed to fish for men of riches.

66. The treasures of the indulgences are nets with which they now fish for the riches of men.

67. The indulgences which the preachers loudly proclaim as the greatest graces are known to be truly such, insofar as they promote gain.

68. Yet in truth they are the very smallest graces compared with the grace of God and the piety of the cross.

69. Bishops and curates are bound to admit the commissaries of apostolic pardons, with all reverence.

70. But they are still more bound to strain with all their eyes and attend with all their ears that these men do not preach their own dreams in place of the commission of the pope.

71. He who speaks against the truth of apostolic pardons, let him be anathema and accursed;

72. But he who guards against the lust and license of the indulgence preachers, let him be blessed.

73. Just as the pope justly thunders[16] against those who, by any art, contrive the injury of the traffic in pardons.

74. Much more does he intend to thunder against those who use the pretext of pardons to contrive the injury of holy love and truth.

75. To think the papal pardons so great that they could absolve a man even if he had committed an impossible sin and violated the mother of God—this is madness.

76. We affirm, on the contrary, that the papal pardons are not able to remove the guilt of the very least of venial sins.

77. The saying that even if St. Peter were now pope, he could not bestow greater graces, is blasphemy against St. Peter and against the pope.

78. We affirm, on the contrary, that both he, and any other pope, has greater graces to grant, namely the Gospel, powers, gifts of healing, etc., as it is written in 1 Corinthians 12[:6, 9, 28].

79. To say [as the preachers of indulgences do] that the cross emblazoned with the papal arms is of equal worth with the cross of Christ is blasphemy.

80. Those bishops, curates, and theologians who allow such talk to be spread among the people will have to render an account for this.

81. This license in preaching of pardons makes it no easy matter, even for learned men, to rescue the reverence due to the pope from slander, or even from the shrewd questionings of the laity.

82. For instance: "Why does not the pope empty purgatory for the sake of holy love and of the dire need of the souls that are there, if he redeems an infinite number of souls for the sake of miserable money spent building a basilica? The former reasons would be most just; the latter is most trivial."

---

[16]   I.e., threatens with the "thunderbolt" of excommunication

83. Again: "Why are funeral and anniversary masses for the deceased continued, and why does the pope not return or permit the withdrawal of the funds bequeathed for this purpose, since it is wrong to pray for those who are already redeemed?"

84. Again: "What is this new piety of God and the pope that for money they allow an impious man and an enemy of God to buy out of purgatory the pious soul of a friend of God, and do not, rather, because of that pious and beloved soul's own need, free it for pure love's sake?"

85. Again: "Why are the penitential canons, long since in actual fact and through disuse abrogated and dead, now redeemed with money by the granting of indulgences, as though they were still alive and in force?"

86. Again: "Why does not the pope, whose wealth is today greater than the wealth of Crassus,[17] build just this one Basilica of St. Peter with his own money, rather than with the money of poor believers?"

87. Again: "What does the pope remit or grant to those who by perfect contrition have a right to full remission and participation?"

88. Again: "What greater blessing could come to the Church than if the pope were to do a hundred times a day what he now does once, and bestow on every believer these remissions and participations?"

89. "Since the pope, by his pardons, seeks the salvation of souls rather than money, why does he suspend the indulgences and pardons granted before now, since these have equal efficacy?"

90. To repress these arguments and scruples of the laity by force alone, and not to resolve them by giving reasons, is to expose the Church and the pope to the ridicule of their enemies and to make Christians unhappy.

---

17 Marcus Licinius Crassus (c. 115 BC–53 BC) amassed an enormous fortune during his life. He is considered to be among the wealthiest men in all of history and has become the prototype of "the rich."

91. If, therefore, pardons were preached according to the spirit and mind of the pope, all these questions would be resolved with ease; no, they would not exist.

92. Away, then, with all those prophets who say to the people of Christ, "Peace, peace!" though there is no peace.

93. Blessed be all those prophets who say to the people of Christ, "Cross, cross!" and there is no cross.

94. Christians should be exhorted to strive diligently to follow Christ, their Head, through penalties, death, and hell;

95. And thus be confident of entering into heaven through many tribulations rather than through the assurance of peace.